27.07

DATE DUE

MAY 0 2 2007	
NOV 0 2 2007	
DEC 0 1 2007	
MAY 0 2 2008	

DEMCO, INC. 38-2931

D1069056

Energy

By Darlene R. Stille

THE CHILD'S WORLD®
CHANHASSEN, MINNESOTA

The Child's World

Published in the United States of America by The Child's World®
PO Box 326, Chanhassen, MN 55317-0326
800-599-READ
www.childsworld.com

Content Adviser:
Mats Selen, PhD,
Professor of Physics,
University of Illinois,
Urbana, Illinois

Photo Credits: Cover/frontispiece: Steve Smith/Corbis. Interior: Bettmann/Corbis: 6, 8, 30-bottom left; Corbis: 7, 10 (Bill Varie), 11 (David Katzenstein), 16 (Patrik Giardino), 25 (Lester Lefkowitz), 26 (Michele Westmorland), 27 (Issei Kato/Reuters NewMedia Inc.), 30-left (Hulton-Deutsch Collection); Getty Images: 4 (The Image Bank/Michael Melford), 30-top right (Hulton|Archive); Getty Images/Stone: 9 (Emmerich & Webb), 17 (Jack Ambrose); Adam Jones/Visuals Unlimited: 15; Photo Researchers: 12 (Michael Lustbader), 13 (George D. Lepp), 14 (Sid Greenberg), 19 (James Stevenson), 22 (Victor de Schwanberg); PictureQuest: 5 (Digital Vision), 18 (Image Source), 21 (Creatas), 23 (Spencer Grant/PhotoEdit), 24 (Joseph Sohm; ChromoSohm/Stock Connection).

The Child's World®: Mary Berendes, Publishing Director

Editorial Directions, Inc.: E. Russell Primm, Editorial Director; Pam Rosenberg, Line Editor; Katie Marsico, Assistant Editor; Matt Messbarger, Editorial Assistant; Susan Hindman, Copy Editor; Susan Ashley, Proofreader; Peter Garnham, Olivia Nellums, and Katherine Trickle, Fact Checkers; Tim Griffin/IndexServ, Indexer; Cian Laughlin O'Day, Photo Researcher; Linda S. Koutris, Photo Selector

The Design Lab: Kathleen Petelinsek, Design; Kari Thornborough, Page Production

Library of Congress Cataloging-in-Publication Data
Stille, Darlene R.
  Energy / by Darlene R. Stille.
     p. cm. — (Science around us)
  Includes bibliographical references.
  ISBN 1-59296-220-3 (lib. bdg. : alk. paper) 1. Power resources—Juvenile literature.
[1. Power resources.] I. Title.
II. Science around us (Child's World (Firm))
  TJ163.23.S775 2005
  621.042—dc22   2003027224

Table of Contents

CHAPTER ONE

DISCOVERING ENERGY

Think about a cold winter morning. You throw off your blankets and hop out of bed. The house is nice and warm. A furnace heats your house. You go to the kitchen and put a slice of bread in the toaster. Up pops a hot piece of toast. Cold winter days are not so bad because you have heat energy.

A very long time ago, **prehistoric** people had only furs and animal skins to keep them warm. They ate seeds, fruits, nuts, and raw

Heat energy produced by a furnace or wood stove will keep a house warm even in the cold of winter.

meat. About 1¹/₂ million years

ago, their lives changed forever.

Prehistoric people began to use

heat energy from fire.

In dry conditions, a bolt of lightening can spark a forest fire.

No one knows how prehistoric

people discovered fire. Maybe a bolt

of lightning set a forest on fire. Maybe the people ate the meat of

animals killed in the forest fire and found it tasted better than

raw meat.

Once they discovered fire, ancient people kept a main fire going

in each village. They made sure the fire did not go out. It was hard

to start a fire before matches were invented.

Prehistoric people used energy from fire to keep warm. They used

the energy from fire to cook their food. Later, people learned how to make iron by heating rocks containing iron ore with fire. They used the iron to make many kinds of tools that helped them to do work.

Ancient people also used the energy of animals. They rode horses and camels. They used oxen to pull carts and wagons.

Life changed again when inventors learned to build steam engines in the 1600s and 1700s. The first steam engines burned wood. Later

Ancient people learned how to use the heat energy of fire to melt metals so that they could be made into tools.

steam engines burned coal.

Heat from the burning wood

or coal made water hot. When

the water got very hot, it

turned into steam. The energy

from this steam could be used

to do many things. Steam

engines ran machines used in

It became much faster and easier to move goods and people from place to place when inventors learned how to harness the energy of steam to power boats.

factories to make furniture, clothes, and other products. Steam engines

turned wheels on **locomotives** to pull trains. Steam engines

turned paddle wheels on riverboats and big **propellers** on the back

of large ships.

In the 1800s, people learned how to make electric energy. Electric

energy makes today's lightbulbs, toasters, microwave ovens, TV sets,

Henry Ford sits in his first automobile. As a boy, he enjoyed tinkering with engines. He completed his first self-propelled vehicle in 1896 and started the Ford Motor Company in 1903.

and computers work. Inventors also made the gasoline engine in the 1800s. Gasoline engines power cars, trucks, and buses. They took the place of animals that pulled wagons.

Scientists have found that energy is one of two main things that make up the universe. The other thing is matter. **Matter** is the stuff that we can see and smell and feel. Energy is what makes matter change or move.

CHAPTER TWO

KINDS OF ENERGY

There are many kinds of energy. Most of the energy you use is heat energy. Air or water heated by a furnace keeps your house warm. Heat from a stove cooks your dinner. Heat energy is also called **thermal** energy.

The heat given off by this gas stove is a form of thermal energy.

We are all familiar with electric energy. Electric energy makes reading lamps and streetlights glow. It keeps the food in your refrigerator cold. It lets you warm snacks in your microwave oven. It lets you play games or do homework on your computer. It brings your favorite shows to the TV set in your home.

Anything that moves also has energy. The energy of motion is called kinetic energy. A thrown baseball has kinetic energy. Moving cars and trucks have kinetic energy. A turning wheel has kinetic energy. You and your friends have kinetic energy when you walk or run or wave your arms.

Electric energy makes it possible for you to play video games on your TV.

Chemical energy makes batteries work. The chemical energy in batteries turns into electric energy that you can carry with you. The electric energy can light up flashlights or make toy trucks zoom around.

The turning wheels of a remote-controlled ruck have kinetic energy.

Your body converts food to energy. Food gives your body energy to work and play. It gives your brain energy to think and learn.

There is energy in the blowing wind. There is energy in water dropping over a waterfall. There is **solar** energy in the rays of heat and light from the Sun.

CHAPTER THREE

WHERE ENERGY COMES FROM

t seems that you can get energy from many different things. But

almost all the energy on Earth comes from the Sun. Rays of heat

and light from the Sun keep Earth warm. Without this solar energy,

there could be no life on Earth.

Almost all of the energy on Earth comes from the Sun.

Plants and animals need the Sun's energy. Green plants use sunlight to make food. Plants give off a gas called oxygen when they make food. All animals must breathe in oxygen to live. In turn, animals give off a gas called carbon dioxide when they breathe out. Plants need that carbon dioxide in order to make food.

Green plants need the energy of the Sun to make food.

Even wood, coal, and gasoline have stored energy that first came from the Sun. Trees are big plants that you can burn to make heat energy. Coal, oil, and natural gas are fossil fuels that you can burn to make energy. Fossil fuels come from the remains of plants and animals that died millions of years ago. The ancient plants and animals that became fossil fuels once used energy from the Sun.

Even the energy in wind and water comes from the Sun. Energy from the Sun heats air above Earth and makes the wind blow. It heats lakes, oceans, and rivers so that water evaporates, or goes into, the air. The water falls back down as rain or snow.

The energy of the Sun heats the water in lakes, rivers, and oceans on Earth. The water goes into the air and comes back down to Earth in the form of snow or rain.

ENERGY FROM MINES AND WELLS

It takes a lot of coal, oil, and natural gas to make the energy used each day by people all over the world. Coal, oil, and natural gas come from different places on Earth.

Coal comes from mines. Some coal is deep in the ground. Miners make tunnels to dig out the coal. Some coal is close to the surface. Miners strip away soil to get to this coal. Coal gets loaded onto barges or trains. It goes right to power plants or factories, where it is burned.

Oil comes from oil wells drilled down into rock. Some oil wells are on land. Some oil wells are on the bottom of the sea. Oil that comes out of wells is called crude oil or petroleum. Pipes, ships, or tanker trucks carry crude oil to places called refineries.

At a refinery, the thick, gooey crude oil gets changed into the oil used for heating homes and burning in power plants. It gets changed into motor oil that makes engines run smoothly. It gets changed into gasoline that makes cars go. Petroleum is also used to make many kinds of plastics.

Natural gas also comes from wells. Natural gas goes right into pipes that carry the gas to homes, power plants, and factories.

CHAPTER FOUR

STORED AND MOVING ENERGY

D o you wake up in the morning feeling full of energy and ready to go? **Physicists** say that energy is either stored or in motion. All the energy in the universe goes back and forth between stored and in motion.

When you sit very still, your body is full of stored energy. Physicists call this kind of energy potential energy. Your legs are ready to walk or run. Your arms are ready to throw or lift.

A girl jumping on a bed demonstrates the energy of motion.

This slingshot has potential energy as long as the boy is holding the stretched-out rubber band. When he lets go, the energy will change to kinetic energy.

You can use a rubber band to see how stored and moving energy work. Pull back on the rubber band. The stretched rubber band has stored energy, or potential energy. Let one end of the rubber band go. The rubber band snaps forward. The rubber band has kinetic energy, or energy of movement, when it goes forward.

Suppose you set a ball on your closet shelf. The ball has potential energy when it is sitting on the shelf. If the ball falls off the shelf, its potential energy changes to kinetic energy.

There are different kinds of kinetic energy. A falling ball moves from one place to another. A wheel goes around and around. A plucked guitar string vibrates back and forth. The ball, the wheel, and the guitar string all have kinetic energy when they are moving.

A pendulum shows how energy keeps changing between stored and moving energy. A pendulum is a long rod with a heavy disk or tube on the end. Grandfather clocks have pendulums that swing back and forth. At the top of its swing, when it can go no higher, the pendulum has only potential

When you pluck a guitar string you give it the energy of movement, or kinetic energy.

energy. Then the pendulum starts to swing back the other way. At the lowest point of its swing, when the pendulum looks like it is straight up and down, it has only kinetic energy. At the top of its swing the other way, the energy becomes potential energy. From potential, to kinetic, to

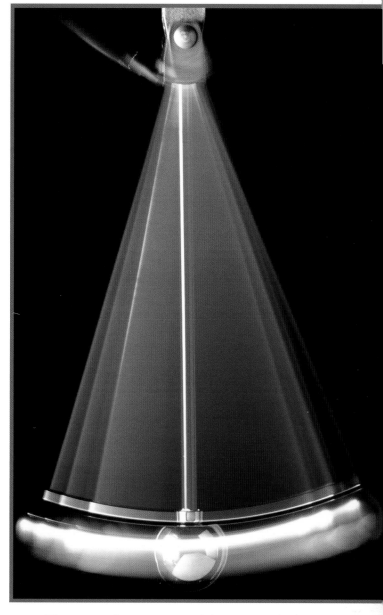

The energy of a swinging pendulum constantly changes back and forth from potential to kinetic energy.

potential energy again, the pendulum swings back and forth.

CHAPTER FIVE

HOW ENERGY CAN CHANGE

Scientists say that the amount of energy in the universe never changes. It is always the same. This is called the law of conservation of energy. But one kind of energy can change into another kind of energy. These changes happen all the time.

Heat energy can be used to make things move, giving them kinetic energy. You can see how this works in a steam engine. You burn wood or coal to make heat energy. The heat energy makes water hot enough to boil and turn into steam. The steam pushes on a rod in a tube called a piston and makes the piston move. The heat energy in the steam makes kinetic energy in the piston. The piston and other parts attach to a wheel and make the wheel go around. Pistons and wheels are used in many kinds of machines.

Several different changes in energy take place in power plants.

Heat energy is created by burning coal, oil, or natural gas. Some

power plants make heat from nuclear energy, the energy inside tiny

bits of matter called atoms.

The heat turns water into

steam. The steam pushes on

turbines that look a little

like giant fan blades. This

makes the turbines spin.

The spinning turbines have

kinetic energy. The kinetic

energy from the turbines

makes a machine called

an electric generator work.

Energy goes through several changes at a power plant to produce the electrical energy that we use in our homes and factories.

Windmills harness the energy of the wind so that it can be used to make electricity.

The generator turns mechanical energy into electrical energy.

Other kinds of energy are used in power plants. The kinetic energy of water falling over a dam can turn the blades of a turbine. The kinetic energy in wind can turn the blades of a **windmill.**

The energy in falling water or blowing wind is used to make electrical energy inside some power plants.

Electric energy is sent out from the power plant on wires. The wires go to your home. Electric energy can go into your toaster. The toaster changes electric energy to heat energy. The heat turns your bread into a nice, hot slice of toast.

FRICTION AND HEAT

The energy of motion can change into heat energy. This change happens when two surfaces rub together. The rubbing creates something called friction. Friction turns the kinetic energy of moving parts into heat energy.

Long ago, people rubbed sticks together to make fire. Friction from rubbing made the sticks hotter and hotter. Finally, one stick began to smoke. Grown-ups still use friction to make fire. Striking a match against a matchbox creates friction. Heat from the friction makes the match catch on fire.

Sometimes friction is bad. It wastes energy by turning the mechanical energy made by machines into unwanted heat. The heat comes from moving parts rubbing together. The heat can damage parts in a machine. You can put oil on moving parts to cut down on friction and heat.

Sometimes friction is useful. The brakes on your family car use friction to slow or stop the wheels from turning. If you could feel the brakes and wheels, you would find that they are hot. Friction from brakes rubbing against wheels changes the kinetic energy of the turning wheels into heat energy.

CHAPTER SIX

ENERGY AND POLLUTION

Cars and buses let you travel to many places. Trucks deliver food, clothing, furniture, and most of the other things you use every day. Most cars, trucks, and buses burn fossil fuels.

It is hard to imagine life without the electric energy that comes from power plants. Most electric power plants also burn fossil

Cars convert the energy from fossil fuels into the energy of movement so that we can easily travel from one place to another.

fuels. Steel mills, automobile plants,

and most other factories all

burn fossil fuels.

Fossil fuels give off fumes

and gases when they burn.

The fumes and gases pollute

the air. Some pollution is a

haze called smog. Breathing

*Fumes from fossil fuels pollute our air
and damage our environment.*

smog is bad for your health. Some pollution falls as acid rain. Acid rain

can kill trees in forests and fish in lakes.

Gases from burning fossil fuels may be changing Earth's climate.

Power plants and factories give off carbon dioxide and other gases

called greenhouse gases. Greenhouse gases trap heat from the Sun.

The gases work like the glass walls and ceiling of a greenhouse. Too

Some scientists think that the gases given off by burning fossil fuels are slowly changing Earth's climate. They believe that some places may eventually turn into dry deserts.

much carbon dioxide in the air around Earth could trap too much heat from the Sun and make Earth warmer. Some scientists think that this could eventually make some places turn to dry deserts. Other places might be flooded with too much rain.

Scientists and engineers are looking for ways to make energy without pollution. They are also looking for ways to save energy. You could help by riding in car pools and on trains or buses. Turn off lights when you leave a room. Doing little things to save energy could make a big difference.

COOL NEW CARS

Engineers are trying to make cars that use less gasoline and give off less pollution. The newest type of car that you can buy gets energy from both batteries and gasoline. These cars are called hybrids. Batteries in a hybrid run an electric motor. Gasoline runs a small engine that can both power the car and charge the batteries. Hybrids even harness the energy of stopping the car to recharge the batteries. Friction would otherwise waste the energy by turning it into heat. The gas engine turns on and off to save energy.

Scientists are looking at other ways to make energy for cars. One way is to use fuel cells. A fuel cell is like a battery. It changes chemical energy into electricity. The gases hydrogen and oxygen change into water and give off electricity and heat.

Scientists are also looking at solar cells to power cars. Solar cells change sunlight into electricity. Solar cells now make electricity for satellites in space. However, scientists will need to figure out how cars with solar cells can be driven at night.

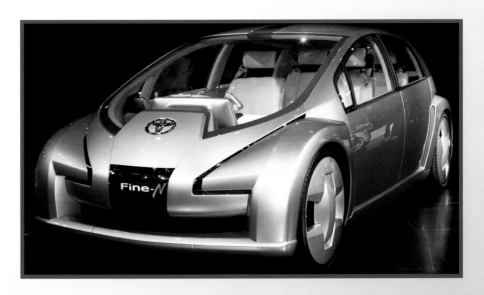

GLOSSARY

chemical (KEM-uh-kuhl) Something that is chemical has to do with the study of substances and what they are made of.

locomotives (loh-kuh-MOH-tivz) Locomotives are the engines that are used to move railroad cars.

matter (MAT-ur) Matter is anything that takes up space and has weight.

physicists (FIH-zih-sists) Physicists are scientists who study matter and energy.

prehistoric (pree-hi-STOR-ik) If something is prehistoric, it has to do with the time before history was recorded in written form.

propellers (pruh-PEL-erz) Propellers are rotating blades that provide a force that moves something through air or water.

solar (SO-lur) Something that is solar has to do with the sun.

thermal (THUR-mul) Something that is thermal has to do with heat.

windmill (WIND-mil) A windmill is a machine that is operated by the power of the wind.

▶ Heat energy goes only one way. It goes from something hot to something colder. When you put ice in your lemonade, it looks like the ice is making your drink colder. Your lemonade is really making the ice warmer.

▶ In 1855, two German engineers made the first gasoline engine that worked well. Their names were Gottlieb Daimler and Wilhelm Maybach. Another German inventor named Karl Benz also invented a gasoline engine that year. Daimler and Benz both started automobile companies. The two companies became the Daimler-Benz Company in 1926. The company made the Mercedes-Benz car.

▶ Scottish inventor James Watt did not invent the steam engine, but he made important improvements to it in the 1700s. Before then, steam engines could only be used to work pumps. Watt made the kind of steam engine that could run factories and make steamboats and locomotives go.

▶ There is hot water deep underground in some places on Earth. The water sometimes shoots up in hot fountains called geysers. Sometimes people use the hot water to make steam. This kind of energy is called geothermal energy. The heat energy in the steam can be used to make electrical energy.

▶ Scientists say that some kinds of energy are renewable. Renewable energy can be used over and over again. Energy from the Sun, from wind, and from falling water is renewable energy. Some energy is nonrenewable. We use up nonrenewable energy faster than Earth can make it. Fossil fuels are nonrenewable energy.

▶ A natural gas leak smells like rotten eggs. But natural gas does not have an odor. Gas companies add the bad smell so that you can tell if there is a dangerous gas leak in your home or school.

▶ Carbon monoxide is a dangerous gas that comes from burning fossil fuels. Automobiles and home furnaces give off carbon monoxide. You cannot see or smell carbon monoxide. That is why it is important to have carbon monoxide detectors in your home. They will sound an alarm if there is a carbon monoxide leak in your home.

TIMELINE

1 MILLION B.C.   Early man learns to control fire.

3000   Mules are used to transport materials in the Middle East. Solar power is used by the Chinese, Romans, Greeks, Egyptians, and Phoenicians to dry crops and to evaporate salt water to produce salt.

1200   Primitive sailboats in Polynesia use wind power as their primary energy source.

1,000–851   People in China are among the first to use coal as fuel.

A.D. 1629   Italian Giovanni Branca invents a simple turbine that uses steam to turn the blades of a wheel.

1712   The first successful steam engine is built in Great Britain by Thomas Newcomen.

1804   A successful steam locomotive is built by Richard Trevithick (top right) in Wales.

1879   Thomas Edison (bottom right) and his team of scientists invent the first practical electric lightbulb.

1938–1939   Otto Hahn (left), Lise Meitner, and Fritz Strassmann discover nuclear fission.

1944   The first nuclear reactor begins operating in Richland, Washington.

1954   The first practical solar cells are created by American scientists.

HOW TO LEARN MORE ABOUT ENERGY

At the Library

Bradley, Kimberly Brubaker, and Paul Meisel (illustrator).
Energy Makes Things Happen. New York: HarperCollins, 2003.

Cooper, Christopher. *Forces and Motion: From Push to Shove.*
Chicago: Heinemann Library, 2003.

Fowler, Allan. *Energy from the Sun.* New York: Children's Press, 1997.

On the Web

VISIT OUR HOME PAGE FOR LOTS OF LINKS ABOUT ENERGY:
http://www.childsworld.com/links.html
Note to Parents, Teachers, and Librarians: We routinely verify our Web links to make
sure they're safe, active sites—so encourage your readers to check them out!

Places to Visit or Contact

AMERICAN MUSEUM OF SCIENCE AND ENERGY
To learn more about energy
300 South Tulane Avenue
Oak Ridge, TN 37830
865/576-3200

TEXAS ENERGY MUSEUM
*To learn more about the history
and science behind petroleum energy*
600 Main Street
Beaumont, TX 77701
409/833-5100

INDEX

About the Author

Darlene R. Stille is a science writer. She has lived in Chicago, Illinois, all her life. When she was in high school, she fell in love with science. While attending the University of Illinois she discovered that she also loved writing. She was fortunate to find a career that allowed her to combine both her interests. Darlene Stille has written more than 60 books for young people.